EXPLORE BIOMES

DESERT BIOMES

BY SARAH WILSON GREGORY

Kids Core

An Imprint of Abdo Publishing
abdobooks.com

abdobooks.com

Published by Abdo Publishing, a division of ABDO, PO Box 398166, Minneapolis, Minnesota 55439.

Printed in the United States of America, North Mankato, Minnesota.
052023
092023

THIS BOOK CONTAINS RECYCLED MATERIALS

Cover Photo: Shutterstock Images
Interior Photos: Tom McHugh/Science Source, 4–5; Charles T. Peden/Shutterstock Images, 6; Zhukova Valentyna/Shutterstock Images, 8; Shutterstock Images, 10–11, 13 (top left), 13 (bottom left), 14, 28 (kangaroo rat), 29 (fox, hawk); Marie Kaz/Shutterstock Images, 13 (top right); Vladimir Melnik/Shutterstock Images, 13 (bottom right); R. M. Nunes/Shutterstock Images, 16; Wojciech Dziadosz/Shutterstock Images, 18; MerlinTuttle.org/Science Source, 20–21; Denis Tangney Jr./iStockphoto, 22; Vinnikava Viktoryia/Shutterstock Images, 25; BlueRingMedia/Shutterstock Images, 28–29; Alexandr Vectors Pattern/Shutterstock Images, 29 (snake)

Editor: Angela Lim
Series Designer: Ryan Gale

Library of Congress Control Number: 2022949084

Publisher's Cataloging-in-Publication Data

Names: Wilson Gregory, Sarah, author.
Title: Desert biomes / by Sarah Wilson Gregory
Description: Minneapolis, Minnesota: Abdo Publishing Company, 2024 | Series: Explore biomes | Includes online resources and index.
Identifiers: ISBN 9781098291075 (lib. bdg.) | ISBN 9781098277253 (ebook)
Subjects: LCSH: Deserts--Juvenile literature. | Biotic communities--Juvenile literature. | Habitats--Juvenile literature. | Life zones--Juvenile literature. | Desert animals--Juvenile literature. | Desert plants--Juvenile literature. | Desert ecology--Juvenile literature.
Classification: DDC 577--dc23

CONTENTS

Kangaroo rats have strong hind legs.

CHAPTER 1

SURVIVING IN THE DESERT

Afternoons in the desert can be very hot. A kangaroo rat sleeps in its **burrow** during the hottest part of the day. The temperature underground is not as hot as it is at the surface.

Many desert animals rely on cacti as a source of food and water.

The kangaroo rat wakes up when the sun goes down. The desert sands are cooler at night. The kangaroo rat races across the sand. It stops at a cactus and looks for seeds to eat.

Water can be hard to find in the desert. The kangaroo rat can survive with very little water.

It gets moisture from the seeds it eats. It uses the pouches in its cheeks to carry seeds back to its burrow.

About Deserts

Desert biomes are the driest places on the planet. A biome includes the plants and animals that live in the region. It also includes nonliving things, such as soil and weather.

The Driest Place on Earth

Antarctica is the largest desert on Earth. Snowfall is rare there. It receives around 2 inches (5 cm) of **precipitation** each year. But it is covered in snow and ice. Cold temperatures keep the snow from melting.

Dry, sandy soil makes it difficult for plants to grow in some parts of Death Valley in California.

Deserts cover one-fifth of the planet. They can be hot or cold. They can be sandy or rocky. Deserts in Antarctica and the Arctic are cold and have no sand. The Sahara, a desert in Africa, is hot and sandy.

All deserts are very dry. They receive little **precipitation**. In parts of the Atacama Desert in South America, it hasn't rained in more than 500 years! On average, deserts receive less than 20 inches (51 cm) of precipitation each year. The plants and animals that live in deserts must **adapt** to survive with little rainfall.

Further Evidence

Look at the website below. Does it give any new evidence to support Chapter One?

Desert Habitat

abdocorelibrary.com/desert-biomes

Deserts may look different throughout the year. Wildflowers at Joshua Tree National Park usually bloom in the early spring.

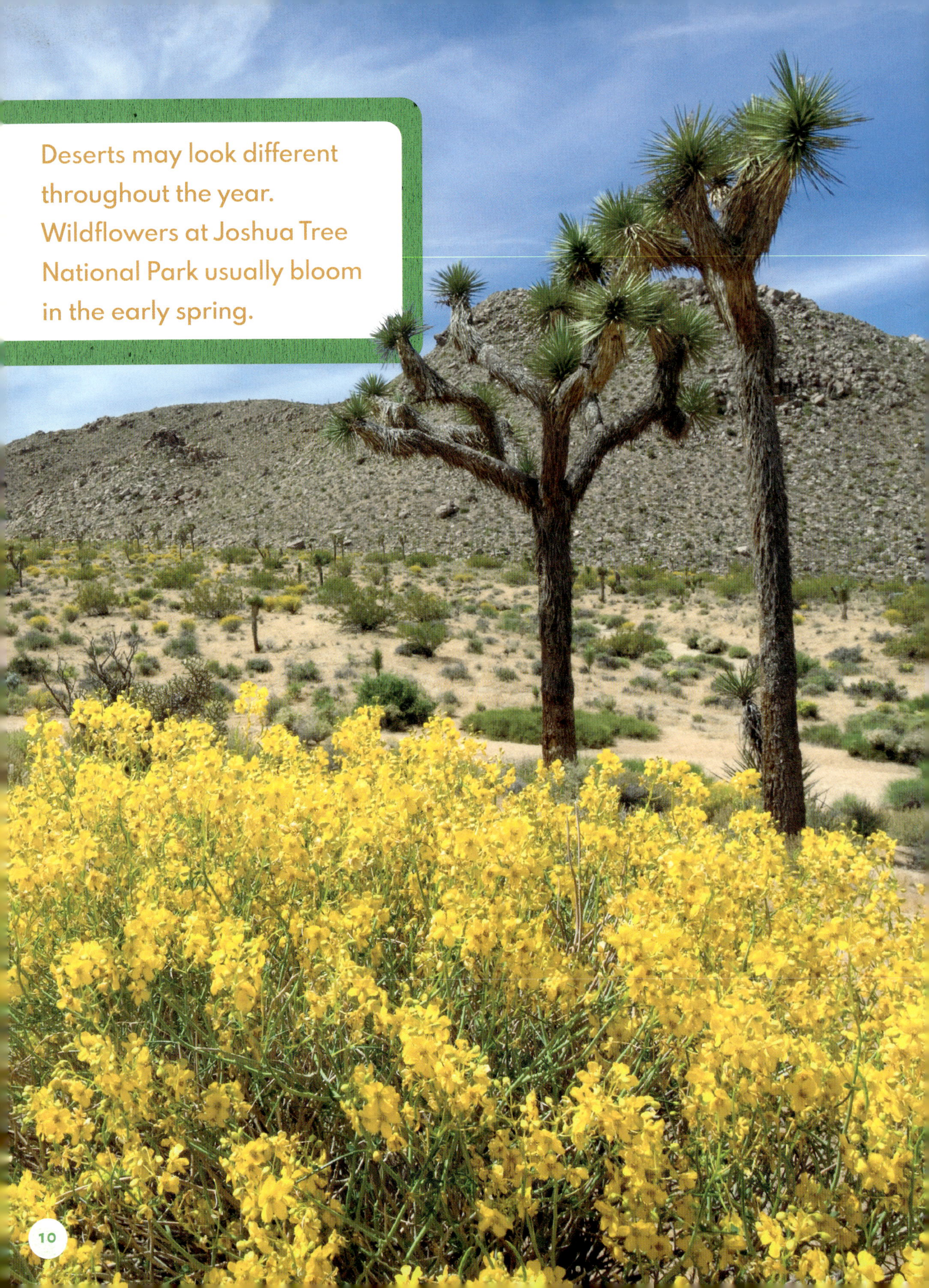

CHAPTER 2

TYPES OF DESERTS

There are four types of deserts. They are hot and dry deserts, **semiarid** deserts, coastal deserts, and cold deserts. They have different temperatures and soil types.

High mountains block rainfall. They form the Great Basin Desert.

These deserts have sandy and rocky soils. Wind and rain shape rock formations in these deserts. Arches and canyons can be found in semiarid deserts. Mesas are mountains with flat tops. They are also seen in these deserts.

Some scientists consider the Great Basin Desert in the United States to be a semiarid desert. It lies next to the Sierra Nevada and the Cascade Mountains. Many semiarid deserts are near mountains. It is difficult for rain clouds to pass over the tall peaks.

Coastal Deserts

Coastal deserts are next to oceans. Ocean currents and wind keep moisture from reaching the desert. Summer temperatures can reach 75 degrees Fahrenheit (24°C). These deserts have cool winters. The average rainfall is 3 to 5 inches (8–13 cm).

Some rocky areas of the Atacama Desert have been compared to the moon's surface.

The Atacama Desert is a coastal desert. It is next to the Pacific Ocean. It is one of the driest deserts in the world. Coastal deserts, including the Atacama Desert, have salty soil.

Cold Deserts

Cold deserts are sometimes called polar deserts. They have cold temperatures for most of the year. Temperatures in some cold deserts fall below −58 degrees Fahrenheit (−50°C). Precipitation in cold deserts usually falls as snow.

The Gobi

Some scientists describe the Gobi in Asia as a cold desert. Winter temperatures drop as low as −40 degrees Fahrenheit (−40°C). But summer temperatures can reach 113 degrees Fahrenheit (45°C). Others think it is a semiarid desert. Nearby mountains block out rain.

Temperatures in the Antarctic have fallen below −125 degrees Fahrenheit (−87°C).

The Arctic is a cold desert. It is the second-largest desert in the world. The Arctic receives less than 10 inches (25 cm) of rain or snow each year. Snow covers some cold deserts, including the Arctic, year-round.

Explore Online

Visit the website below. What new information did you learn about deserts?

Desert Facts

abdocorelibrary.com/desert-biomes

Some bats drink nectar from cacti. The bats help cacti produce fruit.

CHAPTER 3

LIFE IN THE DESERT

It is difficult to live with little precipitation. Extreme temperatures also make desert life hard. Desert animals and plants have special ways to survive.

Some deserts are home to many plants, including succulents, wildflowers, and shrubs.

Plant Life

Plants need water to grow. This makes life in the desert difficult. Cold temperatures in Antarctica also make it hard for plants. Living things called lichens grow in Antarctica. Lichens are similar to plants. Much of the soil in Antarctica is frozen. Lichens do not have roots. They absorb moisture from the air.

Succulents grow in other deserts around the world. Their thick stems and leaves can store a lot of water. Many have waxy coats. This helps keep water inside the plant.

Yuccas are a type of succulent. They have shallow roots that stretch just under the surface. Their root systems can take in a lot of water.

Yucca Moths

Yucca moths and yucca plants need each other to survive. The moths lay their eggs inside yucca flowers. The moths carry pollen as they move between flowers. Yucca plants can make seeds only after pollen is spread.

EXPLORE THE BIOME

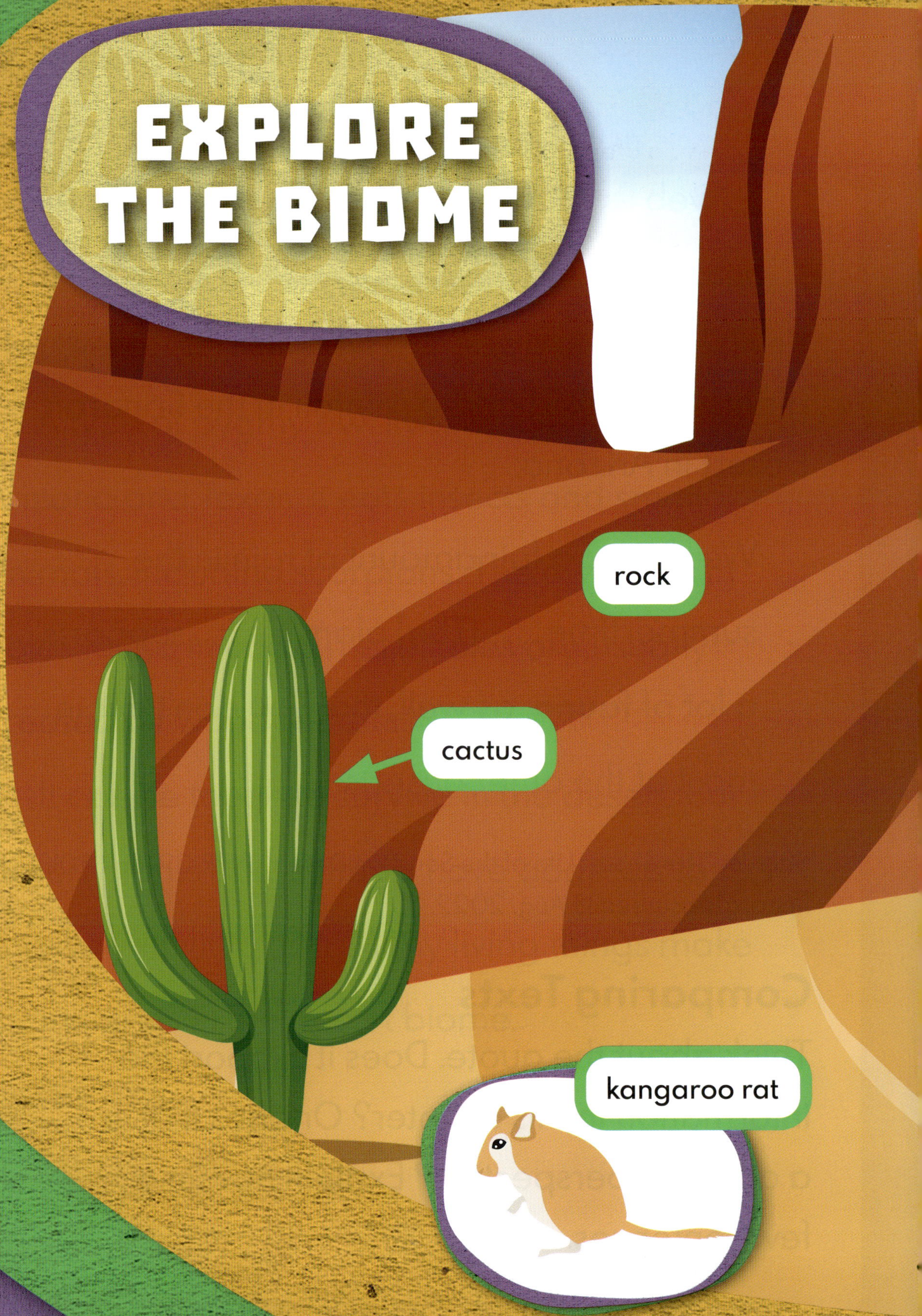

Many plants and animals help make up desert biomes. Can you identify which parts of this desert biome are plants? Which are animals? Can you find any nonliving parts of the biome?

Glossary

adapt
to adjust to survive in a certain biome

burrow
a hole or tunnel dug by an animal

energy
the ability to do work

fauna
animals found within a certain region or area

precipitation
liquid or frozen water that falls from the sky, including rain, sleet, and snow

semiarid
having light rainfall

Online Resources

To learn more about desert biomes, visit our free resource websites below.

Core Library
CONNECTION
FREE! COMMON CORE MULTIMEDIA RESOURCES

Visit **abdocorelibrary.com** or scan this QR code for free Common Core resources for teachers and students, including vetted activities, multimedia, and booklinks, for deeper subject comprehension.

Booklinks
NONFICTION NETWORK
FREE! ONLINE NONFICTION RESOURCES

Visit **abdobooklinks.com** or scan this QR code for free additional online weblinks for further learning. These links are routinely monitored and updated to provide the most current information available.

Learn More

Butterfield, Moira. *Red Planet: Life in Our Deserts and Hot Spots.* 360 Degrees, 2021.

Ridley, Sarah. *Who Ate the Snake? A Desert Food Chain.* Crabtree, 2020.

Index

About the Author

Sarah Wilson Gregory is a former interpretive naturalist and environmental educator. She is a proud wife and mother of three who enjoys reading and writing and (almost!) anything outdoors.